WIN-OR-LOSE SAM

a play in one act

by Sandra Fenichel Asher

Uproar Theatrics

LICENSING & PRODUCTION INQUIRIES
Uproar Theatrics, LLC.
hello@uproartheatrics.com | www.UproarTheatrics.com

Commissioned by The Open Eye Theater

Dedicated to my scattered family:
Weiners in Ohio and IL,
Fenichels in California, NY, and NJ
and Browns in PA,
with a lifetime of love.

WIN-OR-LOSE SAM began its life as WIN-OR-LOSE STANLEY, a commission of The Open Eye Theater, Margaretville, NY, under Producing Artistic Director Amie Brockway. Its summer Youth Theater Workshop production was directed by Elizabeth Sherr. Melonball Choreography was by Mack Oliver. Lighting and sound were designed by Erwin Karl and operated by Billy Mathis. The ensemble cast included Eli Taylor, Saira Faye Pereira, Myah Johnston, Cary Mathis, Laura Walker, Jovan DiDia, Claudia Marinaccio, Carey Mathis, Simone Norwick, Amelia Pascarella, Emma Rotella, Maritsa Stamas, Lillian Taylor, and Madison Tobon. The playwright is grateful to all and cherishes her longtime association with The Open Eye Theater.

WIN-OR-LOSE SAM

CHARACTERS (12+, any gender; cast may be expanded as desired):

SAM, a piglet, gentle, upbeat, and unstoppable

JODY, a young goat, SAM'S friend, loyal, no-nonsense

CASEY, a box turtle, another friend, big-hearted, timid; sometimes confides in audience

BOBBIE, another young goat, a strong leader, but self-important

FRANKIE, a donkey, BOBBIE's pompous assistant

ENSEMBLE
Young farm animals of any fur or feather, enough for two melonball teams: PLAYERS, plus REFEREE(S), and MELON RUNNER(s), as desired. The exact number of PLAYERS, REFEREES, and MELON RUNNERS is left up to the director. There may also be a number of FANS, who may be actors or puppets as animals not playing melonball for their own reasons. Only SAM should remain unchosen even though eager to play. FRANKIE can become a PLAYER, REFEREE, or MELON RUNNER as needed. The following characters are suggestions only. Any favorite farm animals will do. ENSEMBLE lines may be assigned as indicated in the script, divided among additional actors for a larger cast or doubled up for a smaller cast. Creature sounds should be altered appropriately. Audience members may also become active as FANS, perhaps entering and exiting the stands before and after the games and/or pre-learning SAM'S cheer and joining in at SAM'S invitation.

CALF, DUCKLING, FOAL, KITTEN, LAMB, PUPPY,
FANS (optional, real and/or puppet)

TIME: Melonball season, early spring to early fall

PLACE: The Moore Farm. The melonball field takes up
most of the central area, with SAM'S home, a pig pen, to
one side downstage and the penalty pen on the opposite
side. Bleachers may be upstage with some of the audience
seated among FANS and/or actors playing FANS may sit
among the audience.

NOTE: Melonball is a passion for all of these young
animals, so their every-day speech often becomes a rhythmic
cheerleading chant. MUSIC, when called for, can be as
simple as a cowbell or drum beat or a single instrument
played by one of the actors. MELONS may be actual
melons or balls decorated to look like melons or painted
papier mache balls of various sizes. Their heaviness can be
mimed by the actors. Actors playing FANS enter as games
begin and may animate puppets to represent more FANS
and/or be joined by audience members.

*AT RISE: MUSIC. A spring morning on the
Moore Farm. MUSIC fades as ENSEMBLE
enter in pairs and greet one another. SAM is at
home, oblivious to the ENSEMBLE while
working on the third and newest of three charts.*

CALF

Good morning, Duckling!

DUCKLING

Good morning, Calf!

CALF

It's a lovely morning on the Moore Farm –

DUCKLING

It's a melonball morning on the Moore Farm –

CALF

It's a perfect springtime melonball morning –

DUCKLING
(cheerleading --)

Where?

CALF

Right here!

DUCKLING

Right where?

*(CALF and DUCKLING go into cheerleader
mode in rhythmic chanting and gestures, and
ENSEMBLE follows suit as they enter.)*

CALF

Right here . . .
Where we live . . .
And we play . . .
Melonball . . .
Everyday . . .

DUCKLING

All of us together --

CALF

All of us together –

CALF and DUCKLING

All of us together . . .
YAY!
>   *(CALF and DUCKLING move back, chanting
>   softly, as FOAL and KITTEN enter)*
We're the Moore Farm Menagerie . . . the Moore Farm
Menagerie . . . the Moore Farm Menagerie . . .

FOAL

Good morning, Kitten!

KITTEN

Good morning, Foal!

FOAL

It's a lovely morning on the Moore Farm –

KITTEN

It's a melonball morning on the Moore Farm –

FOAL

It's a perfect springtime melonball morning –

                         KITTEN
                 (cheerleading --)
Where?

                          FOAL

Right here!

                         KITTEN

Right where?

                          FOAL

Right here . . .
Where we live . . .
And we play . . .
Melonball . . .
Every day . . .

                         KITTEN

All of us together --

                          FOAL

All of us together --

         CALF, DUCKLING, FOAL, and KITTEN
All of us together . . .
YAY!

                 *(FOAL and KITTEN move back and join CALF
                 and DUCKLING chanting softly as LAMB and
                 PUPPY enter)*

We're the Moore Farm Menagerie . . . the Moore Farm
Menagerie . . . the Moore Farm Menagerie . . .

                          LAMB

Good morning, Puppy!

                                                    3

PUPPY
Good morning, Lamb!

LAMB
It's a lovely morning on the Moore Farm –

PUPPY
It's a melonball morning on the Moore Farm –

LAMB
It's a perfect springtime melonball morning –

PUPPY
(cheerleading --)
Where?

LAMB
Right here!

PUPPY
Right where?

LAMB
Right here . . .
Where we live . . .
And we play . . .
Melonball . . .
Every day . . .

PUPPY
All of us together –

LAMB
All of us together –

CALF, DUCKLING, FOAL, KITTEN, LAMB, and PUPPY
All of us together . . .
YAY!
(softening, as before)
WE'RE THE MOORE FARM MENAGERIE . . . the Moore
Farm Menagerie . . . the Moore Farm Menagerie . . .
(full volume)
All of us together –

CALF

MOO! MOO!

DUCKLING

QUACK! QUACK!

FOAL

NEIGH! NEIGH!

KITTEN

MEOW! MEOW!

LAMB

BAA! BAA!

PUPPY

RUFF! RUFF!

CALF, DUCKLING, FOAL, KITTEN, LAMB, and PUPPY
Where we live . . .
And we play . . .
Melonball . . .
Everyday . . .

CALF

All of us together . . .

CALF, DUCKLING, FOAL, KITTEN, LAMB, and PUPPY
YAY!

>   *(ENSEMBLE freezes in a final cheerleading
>   pose, as JODY crosses stage, in a different space
>   and therefore not seeing them, and reaches
>   SAM'S pen.)*

                              JODY
Good morning, Sam.

                              SAM
                    (barely looking up from his work)
Good morning, Jody.

                              JODY
You do know what day it is, don't you?

                              SAM
Mmm-hmmm. I certainly do.

                              JODY
The first day of spring –

                            STANLEY
The first day of melonball season!

                              JODY
Yes! Everyone's gathering on the field.

                              SAM
I know.

                              JODY
It's almost time for the game --

SAM

I'll be there.

JODY
(peering at chart)
What are you working on?

SAM

A chart.

JODY
Another chart? You already have two . . .

SAM
(steps back and inspects his work for a moment)
This one's different. I'm spelling out the Melonball Rules.
We've never written them down before.

JODY
Great idea! Future generations will need to know!

SAM
Exactly.
(putting the final touch on the current chart)
So . . . there it is, the full history of the Menagerie playing
melonball on the Moore Farm.
(pointing to each chart in turn)
"Moore Farm Menagerie Wins and Losses." "Moore Farm
Menagerie Points and Penalties." And now, "Melonball:
The Official Rules."

> *(MUSIC or SOUND SIGNAL may start with
> each unfreezing and stop with refreezing.
> ENSEMBLE unfreeze and move into positions to
> demonstrate each rule as SAM and JODY read
> from chart.*

ENSEMBLE freezes in each position before moving on to the next. SAM and JODY do not interact with ENSEMBLE, as they're in a different locale, but ALL are unified by knowledge of and devotion to melonball.)

ENSEMBLE
(a cheerleader-style chant as they move into first pose)
Melonball, melonball,
Play it in spring,
Summer and fall.
Morning, evening,
noon or night,
we love to play
and we play it right!
(beat)
Ruuuuuuuuuuuuuule ONE. . . !
(freeze)

SAM
The melonball field must be forty pitchforks long --

JODY
-- measured precisely.

ENSEMBLE
(chanting and moving into next pose)
Melonball, melonball,
Play it in spring,
Summer, and fall.
Morning, evening,
noon or night.
we love to play
and we play it right!
(beat)
Ruuuuuuuuuuuuuule TWO . . . !

(freeze)

SAM
Before each game, one Scooper shall be chosen by a vote of all players.

JODY
The majority wins.

ENSEMBLE
(chanting, same business)
Melonball, melonball,
Play it in spring,
summer and fall.
Morning, evening,
noon, or night,
we love to play
and we play it right.
(beat)
Ruuuuuuuuuuuuuule THREE . . . !
(freeze)

SAM
Each game is played by two teams --

JODY
-- consisting of an equal number of players.

ENSEMBLE

(as they unfreeze, change positions and refreeze a bit faster, holding the extended "Rule" as long as they need to get into place)

Melonball . . . melonball . . .
Play it in spring . . .
Summer . . . and fall.

(beat)
ENSEMBLE (CONT)
Ruuuuuuuuuuuuule FOUR!
(freeze)

SAM
If melons are not available or in season –

JODY
-- ordinary balls of similar size may be used.

ENSEMBLE
(moving into next pose a bit faster)
Morning . . . evening . . .
noon . . . or . . . night.
(beat)
Ruuuuuuuuuuuuule FIVE!
(freeze)

SAM
The Scooper chooses all players –

JODY
-- making sure teams are evenly matched.

ENSEMBLE
(moving into next pose as fast as they can)
We . . . love . . . to . . . play!
(beat)
Ruuuuuuuuuuuuule SIX!
(freeze)

SAM
The Scooper chooses referees --

JODY
and melon runners.

ENSEMBLE
(moving into next pose, demonstrating "fair moves")
We . . . love . . . to . . . play!
(beat)
Ruuuuuuuuuuuuuuule SEVEN!
(freeze)

SAM
Only fair moves may be used to advance the melon toward the goal line or to block the opposing team. The following moves are fair --

JODY
-- nudges . . . pokes . . . punts . . . and passes –

SAM
-- flutters . . . flaps . . . snuffles . . . and snorts.

ENSEMBLE
(moving into next pose, demonstrating "unfair moves" and penalty box)
We . . . love . . . to . . . play!
(beat)
Ruuuuuuuuuuuuuuule EIGHT!
(freeze)

SAM
Unfair moves will result in a two-pitchfork loss for the team and time-out in the Penalty Pen for the misbehaving player. The following moves are unfair --

JODY
-- slaps . . . kicks . . . bites . . . and pecks –

SAM

-- scratches . . . head butts . . . flop-downs . . . and sit-upons.

ENSEMBLE
(moving into next pose, demonstrating "split or squish")
We . . . love . . . to . . . play!
(beat)
Ruuuuuuuuuuuuule NINE!
(freeze)

SAM

A split or squish requires a new melon –

JODY

-- and a do-over.

ENSEMBLE
(next pose, a player crossing the goal line to win)
We . . . love . . . to . . . play!
(beat)
Ruuuuuuuuuuuuule TEN!
(freeze)

SAM

The first team to move the melon over its own goal line –

JODY

-- without a split or squish . . .

SAM and JODY

. . . wins the game!
(SAM and JODY freeze; ENSEMBLE runs cheer again.)

ENSEMBLE

Melonball, melonball,
Play it in spring,
summer, or fall.
Morning, evening,
noon, or night.
We love to play!
We love to play!
We love to play!
          (beat)
And we play it right!
          *(ENSEMBLE freeze in final position. SAM and
          JODY unfreeze.)*

SAM

My favorite game in the world!

JODY

If only you got to play now and then . . .

SAM

Well, there is that little problem.

JODY

If only someone other than Bobbie got to be Scooper now
and then!

SAM

"Rule Two: Before each game, one Scooper shall be chosen
by a vote of all players."

JODY

"The majority wins." I know, I know. But Bobbie *always*
wins the majority!

SAM

Bobbie is big. Bobbie is strong. Bobbie is fast.

JODY

Bobbie is mean! Bobbie is sour as a lemon.

SAM

Bobbie is one squeeze away from lemonade.

JODY

One squeeze away from lemonade? What does that mean?

SAM

It's hard to explain --
> *(Before SAM can explain, CASEY inches on,*
> *gasping for breath --)*

CASEY

Wait for me, Jody!

JODY

Hurry up, Casey. We all need to get to the field. See you
there, Sam!

> *(JODY heads toward ENSEMBLE.)*

CASEY
> *(still inching and gasping --)*
Wait for me, Jody!

JODY

Hurry!
> *(MUSIC as ENSEMBLE unfreezes to admit*
> *JODY and refreezes. MUSIC ends.)*

SAM
> *(puts charts away)*
I'm just about ready to go, Casey.

CASEY

Wait for me, Sam!

SAM

I am waiting for you. I always wait for you.

CASEY

I know.
(to audience)
That's the kind of piglet Sam is.

*(MUSIC. CASEY and SAM exit toward
field. When THEY reach the field, ENSEMBLE
unfreeze, their eyes on BOBBIE, who enters
strutting smugly and followed by FRANKIE,
who is very involved with clipboard and/or other
busy-ness. MUSIC fades.)*

BOBBIE

Frankie!

FRANKIE
(snapping to attention, devotedly)
Yes, Bobbie?

BOBBIE

Line everyone up.

FRANKIE

Yes, Bobbie!

*(blows a whistle or uses another signal
for attention, attempting to get everyone
organized as BOBBIE continues strutting)*

Line up, everyone! Bobbie is about to choose the teams for
this morning's melonball game.

ENSEMBLE

*(all surge forward, bypassing FRANKIE and
waving for BOBBIE'S attention, ad
libbing, interspersed with appropriate creature
SOUNDS)*

Oooh! Oooh! Me, me! Over here, Bobbie! Choose me!

*(JODY, CASEY and SAM also raise their
hands, but with more dignity, though they
are jostled by ENSEMBLE.)*

BOBBIE

Frankie!

FRANKIE

Yes, Bobbie?

BOBBIE

Calm this crew down.

FRANKIE

Yes, Bobbie!
(blows whistle or uses another signal)
Hey! Calm down! Watch it there! Stand still! Stand still or
nobody gets to play!
(ENSEMBLE ignore her, waving and jostling on)

BOBBIE
*(losing patience with ENSEMBLE and
FRANKIE)*

SIT!

*(OTHERS, including FRANKIE, abruptly sit,
wide-eyed and frozen, hands still aloft.)*

Frankie?

FRANKIE
*(stands, struggling to resume pomposity and
devotion)*

Yes, Bobbie.

BOBBIE

Deal with them.
(goes back to strutting)

FRANKIE

Yes, Bobbie.
(to OTHERS)
Hands down!
(Hands go down obediently, in unison.)
Bobbie will choose whomever Bobbie chooses to choose.

JODY
(stands, defiantly)
Hold on there, Frankie! We have not voted for a Scooper
yet. "Rule Two: Before each game, one Scooper shall be
chosen by a vote of all players."

*(faced with pro-and-con mutters from
OTHERS, FRANKIE turns to BOBBIE for
direction --)*

FRANKIE

Bobbie . . . ?

BOBBIE
(shrugs)
Oh, let them vote.

FRANKIE

Yes, Bobbie.
> *(blows whistle or uses another signal)*

All those in favor of Bobbie for Scooper, hands up.
> *(ENSEMBLE hands go up, SAM'S with a shrug,*
> *CASEY'S in response to whatever SAM decides.)*

Hands down.
> *(Hands come down.)*

All against.

> *(JODY'S hand goes up. CASEY sees this and,*
> *confused but wanting to support friends, votes*
> *again.)*

One vote per player!
> *(CASEY timidly lowers hand. To JODY,*
> *sarcastically --)*

I'd call that a majority. Wouldn't you?

JODY

But why is Bobbie always the only one nominated for
Scooper? Why doesn't anybody else ever get a chance to
choose the teams?

CASEY
> *(more an aside to audience than any attempt at*
> *confrontation)*

This is getting my goat!
> *(General ENSEMBLE pro-and-con hub-bub.*
> *FRANKIE turns to BOBBIE --)*

FRANKIE

Bobbie . . . ?
> *(BOBBIE makes the throat-cutting sign to cut*
> *off debate and get on with the proceedings.)*

Yes, Bobbie.

*(FRANKIE blows whistle or uses
another attention-getting signal)*

FRANKIE (CONT)
No, Casey, this is getting OUR goat: Bobbie, to be precise.
Once again, our duly elected Scooper. Right, majority?

ENSEMBLE
Right!

*(MUSIC. FRANKIE leads OTHERS, except for
a doubting and irritated JODY, in a cheer as
BOBBIE passes through the crowd, sizing
everyone up and ultimately choosing two teams
of PLAYERS and moving the rest into position as
REFEREES or MELON RUNNERS. Equipment
is distributed. During this time, FANS, real and/
or puppet, may arrive and take seats in the
stands.)*

FRANKIE
(cheerleading --)
Bobbie the Kid . . . knows us!

OTHERS
Knows us! Knows us!

FRANKIE
Bobbie the Kid . . . shows us!

OTHERS
Shows us! Shows us!

FRANKIE
Bobbie the Kid . . . grows us!

OTHERS

Grows us! Grows us!

FRANKIE

Stronger and stronger . . . every . . . day.

OTHERS

Stronger and stronger. Hip-hip-hooray!

FRANKIE

Go . . . Bobbie!

OTHERS

Go . . . Bobbie!

FRANKIE

Yo . . . Bobbie!

OTHERS

Yo . . . Bobbie!

FRANKIE

Whoa . . . Bobbie!

OTHERS

Whoa . . . Bobbie!

FRANKIE

Bobbie knows –

OTHERS

What Bobbie knows –

FRANKIE

Bobbie leads –

                    OTHERS
Where Bobbie leads.

                    FRANKIE
We all know –

                    OTHERS
We all need –

                    FRANKIE
Bobbie!

                    OTHERS
Go!

                    FRANKIE
Bobbie!

                    OTHERS
Yo!

                    FRANKIE
Bobbie!

                    OTHERS
Whoa!

                    FRANKIE
Bobbie!
                ENSEMBLE
 Bobbie the Kid's our Scooper!
          FRANKIE and OTHERS
YAY!

          *(MUSIC continues under dialogue as long as it
          takes for BOBBIE to mix, match, and arrange*

players, while FRANKIE distributes equipment.
JODY pulls SAM aside; CASEY follows after
them. During the following dialogue, all three
keep one hand raised.)

JODY
Why are you cheering for Bobbie?

SAM
Because Bobbie's our elected Scooper.

JODY
But Bobbie is a bully --

SAM
Rule Two --

JODY
I know Rule Two, Sam!

SAM
Then you know the majority wins. And the majority voted
for Bobbie.

JODY
Some rules are just not fair!

(BOBBIE taps JODY to play on one of the
teams. JODY shrugs BOBBIE off with hand
absent-mindedly still raised.)

SAM
Rules make the game. And we do love the game.
(BOBBIE taps JODY again.)
Don't we?

JODY

(yielding to both SAM and BOBBIE)

Yes, we do love the game.

SAM

Then go play it -- and have fun!

> *(JODY takes her place on a team, to her teammates' delight. BOBBIE taps CASEY, who looks to SAM for guidance.)*

You, too, Casey.

> *(CASEY joins a team, though reluctant to leave SAM. Left to stand alone like the proverbial cheese, SAM remains hopeful and patient, doing whatever he needs to do to keep his tired hand aloft. FRANKIE either "suits up" to be REFEREE/MELON RUNNER or hands out whistles to REFEREES, and melons to MELON RUNNERS. FRANKIE and BOBBIE step back to assess preparations, pointedly ignoring SAM. MUSIC stops.)*

JODY

What about Sam?

BOBBIE

What about Sam?

JODY

Sam is still standing there --

BOBBIE

(to SAM)

Out of the way, runt! Beat it!

(SAM shrugs, puts his hand down.
OTHERS watch the following exchange between
JODY and BOBBIE with intense interest. They
don't join the protest, but they don't laugh,
either. They know any one of them could
become BOBBIE's next victim. CASEY shares
concern in asides to the audience.)

JODY
(to BOBBIE)
Why doesn't Sam ever get to play?

CASEY

Oh, dear!

JODY

All the rest of us get a turn.

CASEY
(hanging well back)
Oh, my!

JODY

At least now and then. When we're not referees or melon
runners --

CASEY

Oh, golly!

JODY

Sam never gets to do anything! Why?

CASEY

Jody is causing trouble! I do not like trouble!
(hides)

FRANKIE

Bobbie . . . ?

BOBBIE

I'll handle this.

FRANKIE

Yes, Bobbie.

BOBBIE
*(circles SAM, smirking. SAM remains calm,
undaunted.)*
Why not Sam? I'll tell you why not Sam. Because Sam's
too small.

SAM
(not arguing, just stating a fact)
I'm getting bigger.

CASEY
(peeking out, meekly, to audience)
That's true . . .

BOBBIE

Sam is too weak.

SAM

I'm getting stronger.

CASEY
(same business --)
That's a fact . . .

BOBBIE

Sam is too slow.

SAM

I'm getting faster.

CASEY
(same business --)
Every day . . .

BOBBIE
And . . . Sam's tail is too curly!

SAM, JODY, and CASEY
What?

*(BOBBIE struts away, laughing
uproariously. FRANKIE also laughs loudly.
ENSEMBLE laugh, weakly.)*

CASEY
(to audience)
THAT'S the kind of kid Bobbie is!
(hides)

JODY
(to BOBBIE)
Sam is smart and good and kind!

CASEY
(peeking out)
That's for sure.
(hides)

JODY
Do you know what I think? I think you're afraid of Sam.

CASEY
(peeks out)
Wow!

(hides)

BOBBIE
That's ridiculous. Why would I be afraid of Sam?

JODY
Because everybody loves Sam, and nobody --

BOBBIE
(pointedly turning away from JODY)

Frankie!

FRANKIE
Yes, Bobbie?

BOBBIE
It's time to play melonball!
(struts away from JODY)

FRANKIE
Yes, Bobbie!

JODY
I'm not finished!

SAM
(heading into the stands)
It's all right, Jody. Don't hold up the game. The fans are
waiting, and I'm the biggest melonball fan of all!
*(SAM sits. JODY shrugs, shakes head, and joins
team.)*

FRANKIE
*(blows whistle or uses another attention-getting
device)*
Play melonball!

(MUSIC. TEAMS, REFEREES, and
MELON RUNNERS line up. A beat, and then
CASEY breaks rank to trudge over and sit beside
SAM. MUSIC stops.)

JODY

Hold on! These teams are NOT evenly matched!

ALL, except FRANKIE and BOBBIE
(A general murmur of agreement and concern)
UH-ohhhhhhhhhhhhh!

FRANKIE
(spots CASEY in the stands)
Casey! What are you doing over there?

CASEY

I'm sitting with Sam.

FRANKIE

But we need your shell for roll-off maneuvers.

CASEY

Thank you. But no, thank you.

SAM

They need you, Casey.

CASEY

You need me, too.

SAM
(grinning)
Well, that's a fact. Always.

JODY
(breaks rank to sit with SAM and CASEY)
Move over, you two.

SAM
But you love to play melonball!

JODY
That's not all I love, Sam.

SAM
Wow. Thanks. Well, the teams are even again!

ALL, as above
(A general murmur of approval and relief.)
Ah-hahhhhhhhhhhh!

FRANKIE
(blows whistle or sounds other signal)
Plaaaaaaaaaay melonball!

> *(MUSIC. TEAMS, REFEREES, and MELON
> RUNNERS embark on an energetic mime
> of melonball maneuvers while SAM, JODY, and
> CASEY lead FANS in reacting to plays. All is
> punctuated by creature SOUNDS. Keep in
> mind that melons are both heavy and fragile and
> must be handled gingerly to avoid a split or
> squish. REFEREES keep an eye out for this,
> blow their whistles accordingly, and signal
> MELON RUNNERS to replace melons as
> needed. Occasionally, TEAM
> MEMBERS executing illegal maneuvers are sent
> to the penalty box briefly and their team loses
> ground. After a while, MUSIC slows down and
> softens; melonball game continues in slow*

motion and silence until it freezes under the
following dialogue.)

JODY

So here you are again, Sam – watching.

CASEY

And again and again and again and again --

SAM

I don't mind. And right now, you're both watching with me.
That's pleasant!

JODY

But sometimes we get to play. Everyone gets a turn --
except you.

SAM

I love watching melonball games.

JODY

But you'd rather play.

SAM

That would be good, too. Now and then.

JODY

At least!

SAM

Now and then would be fine.

CASEY

More would be better.

JODY

More would be better than never! Never is not fine!

SAM

Let's just watch the game, okay? Watching is fun. I love
everything about melonball.

JODY

We all do!

CASEY

(to audience)
Everything except Bobbie!

> *(MUSIC changes as melonball game becomes a
> series of tableaux illustrating the
> following situations and establishing the
> passage of time. JODY, CASEY, PLAYERS,
> REFEREES, MELON RUNNERS, and FANS
> change places between tableaux, but BOBBIE is
> always a PLAYER and SAM is always a FAN.
> JODY and CASEY speak their lines from
> whatever position they've assumed, which varies
> -- PLAYER, REFEREE, MELON RUNNER, or
> FAN.)*

JODY

And so Sam watched --

CASEY

-- and watched and watched and watched and watched.

JODY

He watched in sunshine --

CASEY

in wind --

JODY

and in rain.

CASEY

He watched when the Menagerie played one another –

JODY

 -- and he watched when the Menagerie played other farm
teams.

> *(The switch to another farm team may involve*
> *additional actors or indicated by half*
> *the players -- not those on BOBBIE'S side --*
> *changing into different colored hats or other*
> *costume bits.)*

JODY

He watched the team win.

CASEY

He watched the team lose.

JODY

He watched the team tie.

CASEY

He watched and watched and watched and watched.

JODY
(as she and CASEY rejoin SAM)
And whenever he watched –

CASEY

 -- he cheered!

> *(At this point, the tableau shows the other farm*
> *team PLAYERS on the verge of triumph and*
> *Menagerie PLAYERS down in the dumps. ALL*
> *PLAYERS remain frozen. MUSIC fades.)*

SAM
(enthusiastically, with cheerleading moves,
although no one is joining in.)
Horse! Goat! *BULL*, cow, cow!
EWE, nanny, *EWE*, chicken,
hog, hog, *SOWWWWWW!*
Moore Farm Menagerie –
Wow! Wow!
(waving arms and jumping up and down --)
WOWWWWWW!
(looks around, realizes the lack of enthusiasm,
but remains undaunted.)
It's easy to cheer when the Menagerie is winning, but when
they're losing is when they need us most. *Everybody!*

(JODY and CASEY join in, as do other FANS,
including audience.)

SAM, JODY, CASEY, and FANS
Horse! Goat! *BULL*, cow, cow!
EWE, nanny, *EWE*, chicken,
hog, hog, *SOWWWWWW.*
Moore Farm Menagerie –
Wow! Wow!
(waving arms and jumping up and down --)
WOWWWWWW!

(MUSIC. PLAYERS finish up one more play in
which BOBBIE maneuvers the melon over the
finish line, winning the game for the Menagerie.
MUSIC fades. PLAYERS playing the other team
switch back their hats or costume bits to join in
the general rejoicing.)

33

SAM

See? We won! Cheering helps! Fans matter! Great game,
Menagerie! Nice try, Visitors!

> *(MUSIC. ALL exit, including FANS, with good
> cheer, backslapping, fist-bumping, and
> appropriate creature sounds. SAM heads
> home, followed by CASEY, who observes with
> appreciation while SAM gets to work on charts.
> MUSIC fades.)*

CASEY

So what have we got today, Sam?

SAM

Correct me if I'm wrong, please . . .
> *(entering data on charts)*
One win – by the Menagerie.

CASEY

Check.

SAM

One melon-over – by Bobbie.
Two penalty warnings – to Bobbie.

CASEY

Check. Check.

SAM

Three penalties – on Bobbie.
A squish – by Bobbie.
A split – by Bobbie.

CASEY

Check. Check. Check.

                              SAM

Plus . . .
                    (multiple, rapid-fire data entering on charts --)
. . . assists . . . passes . . . reversals . . . and saves – by players
who are NOT Bobbie.

                             CASEY

Check. Check. Check. Check.

                              SAM
                    (steps back, looking at charts)
Bobbie does a lot, but not everything. No one wins alone!

                             CASEY
                        (to audience --)
Try telling Bobbie that!

                    (MUSIC. LIGHTS fade. Time passes.
                    LIGHTS come up on a summer morning.
                    Another gathering of ENSEMBLE while SAM is
                    at home, putting the finishing touches on
                    the latest data entries. CALF, DUCKLING,
                    FOAL, KITTEN, LAMB and PUPPY enter in
                    turn --)

                             CALF

Good morning Duckling!

                           DUCKLING

Good morning, Calf!

                             FOAL

Good morning, Kitten!

                            KITTEN

Good morning, Foal!

LAMB

Good morning, Puppy!

PUPPY

Good morning, Lamb!

CALF

It's a lovely morning on the Moore Farm –

FOAL

It's a melonball morning on the Moore Farm –

LAMB

It's a perfect summertime melonball morning --

(ENSEMBLE cheer together --)

DUCKLING and CALF

Where?

KITTEN and FOAL

Right here!

PUPPY and LAMB

Right where?

DUCKLING, CALF, KITTEN, and FOAL

Right here --
Where we live
And we play
Melonball
Every day!

PUPPY and LAMB

All of us together --

CALF, DUCKLING, FOAL, KITTEN, LAMB, and PUPPY
All of us together –

CALF

MOO! MOO!

DUCKLING

QUACK! QUACK!

FOAL

NEIGH! NEIGH!

KITTEN

MEOW! MEOW!

LAMB

BAA! BAA!

PUPPY

RUFF! RUFF!

CALF, DUCKLING, FOAL, KITTEN, LAMB, and PUPPY
Where we live . . .
And we play . . .
Melonball . . .

CALF, DUCKLING, FOAL, KITTEN, LAMB, and PUPPY
Everyday . . .

CALF

All of us together --

CALF, DUCKLING, FOAL, KITTEN, LAMB, and PUPPY
YAY!
        (beat)
We're the Moore Farm Menagerie . . . the Moore Farm
Menagerie . . . the Moore Farm Menagerie . . .

(ENSEMBLE freezes in a final cheerleading pose. JODY enters and crosses to SAM's pen, as before.)

JODY

Good morning, Sam.

SAM

Good morning, Jody.

JODY

Going to be another hot one today.

SAM

Mmmm-hmmmm. It's summertime.

JODY

Everyone's gathering on the field.

SAM

I know.

JODY

It's almost time for the melonball game.

SAM

I'll be right there.

JODY

(peering at chart)

What are you working on now?

SAM
(indicating chart)
Look! One, two, three, four, five, six, seven, eight, nine,
TEN! Ten wins in a row in our weekend games against other
farm teams! Go, Menagerie!

JODY
That is impressive.

SAM
And you played in games three, five, and nine. Go, you!

JODY
Thanks. But I feel bad that you didn't get to play in a single
one of those games.

SAM
I got to watch.

JODY
Anybody can watch!

SAM
I know! Isn't it wonderful?

JODY
How can you think that -- ?

SAM
(shrugs)
My cup is half-full.

JODY
What cup? Half full of what? What does that mean?

SAM
It's hard to explain --

(Before SAM can explain, CASEY inches on --)

CASEY

Wait for me, Jody!

JODY

Hurry up, Casey! We need to get to the field. See you there, Sam!
(She heads toward ENSEMBLE.)

CASEY

Wait for me, Jody.

JODY

Hurry!

(MUSIC as she joins ENSEMBLE on field and freezes. MUSIC fades.)

SAM
(puts charts away)
I'm about ready to go, Casey.

CASEY

Wait for me, Sam!

SAM

I am waiting for you. I always wait for you.

CASEY

I know.
(grins at audience)
That's the kind of piglet Sam is.

(MUSIC. ENSEMBLE unfreeze. SAM and CASEY join group gathering around

BOBBIE as FRANKIE gets things organized.
BOBBIE still struts, but not so smugly. Seems
troubled. MUSIC fades.)

BOBBIE

Frankie!

FRANKIE

Yes, Bobbie?

BOBBIE

Announce my announcement!

FRANKIE

Yes, Bobbie.
                    (blows whistle or uses another attention-getting
                    sound)
Gather 'round, everyone! Bobbie has an important
announcement to make.

                    (Creature SOUNDS dotted with ad libs of
                    curiosity as OTHERS gather.)

KITTEN

What sort of important announcement?

FRANKIE

Settle down and you'll find out.
                    (hubbub continues with creature SOUNDS)
Settle down! I said, settle down!

BOBBIE

                    (losing patience, as before)

SIT!

                    (ALL except BOBBIE abruptly sit, wide-eyed. A
                    beat, then --)

Frankie?

FRANKIE
(stands, as before)
Yes, Bobbie. I am pleased to announce that Bobbie will now make an announcement.
(BOBBIE clears throat pointedly)
An *important* announcement.

(FRANKIE sits; OTHERS relax but pay attention to BOBBIE, who takes a moment to strut, pleased with the attention, yet concerned. Making the most of the moment, BOBBIE slowly reveals a sheaf of papers.)

DUCKLING
What's all that stuff?

BOBBIE
It's an invitation.

PUPPY
An invitation to what?

BOBBIE
(clears throat and reads--)
"In appreciation of the Moore Farm Menagerie's recent ten-game winning streak, the National Melonball Commission hereby invites the Moore Farm Menagerie to apply for participation in the upcoming Fruit Bowl Tournament."

FOAL
The Fruit Bowl?

CALF
Isn't that the big-time melonball tournament way over yonder?

42

                          BOBBIE
That's the one.

                    (OTHERS jump to their feet in a general hubbub
                    of excitement in creature SOUNDS and ad
                    libbed words: "The Fruit Bowl!" "Wow!"
                    "How exciting!" and so on.BOBBIE signals to
                    FRANKIE to get everyone settled down again.)

                          FRANKIE
There's more! Settle down! I said, settle down!
                    (No response.)

                          BOBBIE
                    (as before)
SIT!
                    (OTHERS sit obediently, as before. A beat,
                    then--)
Frankie?

                          FRANKIE
                    (standing)
Yes, Bobbie.
                    (to OTHERS)
Thank you for your attention. Bobbie will now continue.
                    (She sits.)

                          BOBBIE
There is . . . a problem.

                          DUCKLING
How can there be a problem?

                          KITTEN
This is a great honor!

PUPPY

When's the tournament?

LAMB

When do we leave?

BOBBIE
(holding out a hand to silence the questions)
Not so fast. We're *invited to apply*.
(indicating all the other pages)
The application is long, and it's complicated.

CALF

Ah, you'll figure it out, Bobbie.

BOBBIE

I've already figured it out.

CALF

Good!

BOBBIE

Not so good.
(reading from papers)
To qualify for participation in the Fruit Bowl Tournament,
each team must send in its complete <u>statistics</u>.

LAMB

Its sta-<u>*what*</u>-sticks?

BOBBIE

Sta<u>*tis*</u>tics. That means <u>facts</u>.
(shuffling pages)
Points and penalties for each player. Wins and losses for the
team.

DUCKLING

We win a lot!

PUPPY

That's a fact!

BOBBIE

Not exactly.
(pointing at pages)
We need *numbers* – numbers that prove we've been playing
long and hard. Rain or shine. Win or lose.

FOAL

Numbers! Whoa . . .

LAMB

We don't do numbers.

KITTEN

We just play.

BOBBIE

If we don't have our numbers, we can't fill out the
application.

DUCKLING

Does this mean we can't go to the Fruit Bowl?

BOBBIE

Looks that way. Unless somebody remembers all the
numbers we never wrote down.

> *(General hubbub as before, with animal sounds*
> *plus ad libs of "Numbers?" "Statistics?" "I've*
> *never even heard of statistics" and so on.)*

LAMB

Ten is a number. We've won ten games in a row.

BOBBIE

Ten is a number, but it's only one number.
(waving pages)
We need more. A lot more! We need the full history of the
Menagerie playing melonball on the Moore Farm.

> *(ENSEMBLE begin to shuffle off, shaking their
> heads and murmuring regrets.)*

CALF

Sure wish I could help you, Bobbie.
(exits)

DUCKLING

Sorry, Bobbie.
(exits)

KITTEN

Me, too, Bobbie.
(exits)

FOAL

Numbers! Whoa . . .
(exits)

PUPPY

RRRRUFF luck.
(exits)

LAMB
(turns back to FRANKIE and BOBBIE)
We can go on playing here at home, can't we?

FRANKIE

Sure, we can . . . can't we?

BOBBIE

Yeah, we can go on playing here at home. But it won't be the same. Every time we get out on this field, we'll be thinking about how we missed our chance to go to the big-time Fruit Bowl Tournament.

FRANKIE

You're right. We'll keep thinking "We coulda gone."

LAMB

"We shoulda gone."

BOBBIE

But we can't go, because we don't have our numbers.

FRANKIE

We won some games. We lost some games.

BOBBIE

But how many wins? How many losses?

LAMB

Maybe if we tried really hard, we could remember?
            (LAMB tries really hard, while BOBBIE and
            FRANKIE watch, doubtful and yet hoping --)
Nah.

FRANKIE

What are we going to do?

BOBBIE

There's nothing we can do.

LAMB

So, it's final then? We can't go? Because of numbers?

FRANKIE

Yes. Our statistics. Our long-lost statistics

LAMB

I didn't know we ever had statistics!

BOBBIE

We don't. No statistics. No Fruit Bowl. Nothing.
*(LAMB shakes head and exits sadly. A beat,
then SAM approaches BOBBIE.)*

SAM

Um . . . Bobbie?

BOBBIE

Out of the way, runt.
(starts off, head low)

SAM

(calling after BOBBIE)
But I do have the complete –

BOBBIE

(over the shoulder)

Beat it.

(exits)

SAM

(turning to FRANKIE)
But I have everything –

FRANKIE

Bobbie has spoken!
(exits after BOBBIE)

SAM
(to JODY and CASEY)
But I have –

JODY
We know what you have, Sam.

CASEY
The full history of the Menagerie playing melonball on
Moore Farm.

SAM
Yes! On the charts in my pen.

JODY
They don't care what you have. They don't want to know.

SAM
(puzzled, but not down)
I guess not.

CASEY
(to audience)
Their loss.

*(MUSIC. JODY, SAM, and CASEY
exit, consoling one another. Time
passes. LIGHTS dim and MUSIC takes on a
dirge-like tempo as CALF, DUCKLING, FOAL,
KITTEN, LAMB and PUPPY drag themselves on
to begin an autumn day . . .)*

CALF
Good morning, Duckling . . .

DUCKLING
It's an awful morning, Calf!

FOAL
Good morning, Kitten . . .

KITTEN
It's a miserable morning, Foal!

LAMB
Good morning, Puppy . . .

PUPPY
It's an awful, miserable, autumn melonball morning!

DUCKLING and CALF
(a dispirited mocking of their former cheer --)
Where?

KITTEN and FOAL
Right here!

LAMB and PUPPY
Right where?

CALF, DUCKLING, FOAL, and KITTEN
Who cares
Where we live
And we play
Melonball
Every day?

DUCKLING
All of us unhappy . . .

CALF, DUCKLING, FOAL, KITTEN, LAMB, and PUPPY
All of us unhappy . . .

                              CALF
MOO-OO-OO-OO!

                            DUCKLING
QUA-AAA-AAACK!

                              FOAL
NEEEEEEEEEEIGH!

                             KITTEN
MEEEEEEEEE-OW!

                              LAMB
BAAAAAAAAAAH!

                             PUPPY
AHHHHHH-WOOOOO!

    CALF, DUCKLING, FOAL, KITTEN, LAMB, PUPPY
PHOOOOEY!

                    *(THEY console one another, ignoring BOBBIE
                    and FRANKIE as they, too, drag themselves
                    onstage, also despondent.)*

                             BOBBIE
Frankie?

                            FRANKIE
Yes, Bobbie?

                             BOBBIE
Start the game.

FRANKIE
(a deep sigh, then --)
Yes, Bobbie.
(Blows whistle or uses another attention-getting device. ENSEMBLE look up with no interest.)
Play melonball!

(ENSEMBLE groan in unison, shift positions slightly and sink into an unhappy freeze. FRANKIE and BOBBIE give up and sink with them. JODY and CASEY enter and stand left and right. SAM takes a seat in the stands. FANS may also shuffle into the stands, without enthusiasm.)

JODY
So Sam went on watching.

CASEY
Sam watched the Menagerie play sadly.

ENSEMBLE, FRANKIE and BOBBIE
(as tableau unfreezes and shifts slightly)
We coulda gone . . . we shoulda gone . . .
(freeze)

JODY
Sam watched the Menagerie play madly.

ENSEMBLE, FRANKIE, and BOBBIE
(as tableau unfreezes and shifts again)
But we can't go . . . 'cause we don't know . . .
(freeze)

CASEY
Sam watched the Menagerie play badly.

ENSEMBLE, FRANKIE, and BOBBIE
(as tableau unfreezes and shifts again)
Our numbers . . . our numbers . . . our numbers . . .
(freeze)

JODY

And in spite of all that –

CASEY

Sam cheered!

SAM
(in a valiant effort to raise spirits)
Horse! Goat! *BULL*, cow, cow!
EWE, nanny, *EWE*, chicken,
hog, hog, *SOWWWWWW."*
Moore Farm Menagerie –
Wow! Wow!
(waving arms and jumping up and down --)
WOWWWWWWW!

*(ENSEMBLE groan loudly and drag themselves
off. BOBBIE and FRANKIE start off after
them.)*

SAM

Ah . . . Bobbie?

BOBBIE

Out of the way, runt.
(continues off, head low)

SAM
(calling after BOBBIE)
But I have the complete --

BOBBIE
                    (from offstage)
Beat it.

                      SAM
                  (to FRANKIE)
But I have everything –

                    FRANKIE
Bobbie has spoken!
                  (exits after BOBBIE)

                      SAM
              (to JODY and CASEY)
But I have –

                      JODY
We know what you have, Sam.

                     CASEY
The full history of the Menagerie playing melonball on
Moore Farm.

                      JODY
We know, but they don't want to know. Give up, Sam.
Everyone else has.

                      SAM
                  (undaunted)
But they *should* want to know --

                     CASEY
Their loss.
                  *(JODY and CASEY exit, shaking their heads and
                  consoling one another.)*

54

SAM
(to their disappearing backs --)
I don't want to give up!
(to audience)
I don't want it to be their loss! Melonball is my favorite
game in the whole wide world, and the Moore Farm
Menagerie is my home team!
(beat)
I guess it's all up to me!

> *(MUSIC. Infused with determination, SAM pulls
> himself up as tall as he can and marches back
> and forth three times, carrying charts from home
> to field. SAM props up each chart facing
> upstage, hiding their information. Their backs
> are decorated with lemons. Satisfied, SAM
> sits, ready to watch another game and support
> the team. ENSEMBLE drag themselves on
> again, as do BOBBIE and FRANKIE. They
> create a series of tableaux to illustrate the
> following narrative. MUSIC fades as JODY and
> CASEY enter, see SAM, shrug in resignation,
> and join him.)*

JODY
So Sam went on watching.

CASEY
And watching and watching and watching and watching.

JODY
Sam watched the Menagerie wishing they could go to the
Fruit Bowl.

FOAL
(stirring tableau, then quickly refreezing)
I wish we could go to the Fruit Bowl.

JODY

Sam watched the Menagerie blaming Bobbie for not writing down the facts.

KITTEN
(same business)
I blame Bobbie for not writing down the facts.

CASEY

Sam watched the Menagerie lose again.

JODY

And again.

CASEY

And again and again and again and again.

ENSEMBLE, BOBBIE, and FRANKIE
(same business)
Our numbers . . . our numbers . . . our numbers . . .

CASEY

But he still cheered –

SAM
(still hoping to energize the team)
Horse! Goat! *BULL*, cow, cow!
EWE, nanny, *EWE*, chicken,
hog, hog, *SOWWWWWW."*
Moore Farm Menagerie –
Wow! Wow!
(waving arms and jumping up and down --)
WOWWWWWW!

(Again, ENSEMBLE, BOBBIE, and FRANKIE groan and start to walk off.)

SAM
(with surprising forcefulness)

Wait!

(OTHERS stop short, amazed.)

BOBBIE

Out of the way, runt!

SAM

No!

(OTHERS gasp.)

CASEY

Oh, dear!

BOBBIE

Beat it!

SAM

Uh-uh!

CASEY
(cringing)

Uh-oh!

FRANKIE

Bobbie has spoken!

SAM

I know. I heard him.

JODY
(rushes to SAM'S side)
Sam the Piglet has also spoken!

(OTHERS gasp.)

CASEY
(backing away)
Oooooooh, golly!
(in spite of fear, goes to SAM'S side)

SAM
(drawing up to full height, such as it is)
And . . . I . . . will . . . not . . . *budge* . . . until you *listen*!

*(OTHERS gasp, even more audibly, then
murmur among themselves in creature SOUNDS
of alarm and astonishment. SAM pulls himself
up even taller, if that's possible. JODY and
CASEY do likewise.)*

FRANKIE
Settle down! Settle down!
(The hubbub continues.)

SAM
SIT!

*(ALL OTHERS abruptly sit and listen up,
astounded. SAM paces, with just a touch of self-
confident strut.)*

I, Sam the Piglet, have been thinking. I have been thinking
about melonball – the game I love. I have been thinking
about the Moore Farm Menagerie – my home team. And I
have been thinking about Bobbie the Kid, who has never let
me play – and won't even let me get a word in edgewise. As
a result of all of this thinking, I have made a decision. I have
decided that the time has come for me to gather up all of my

SAM (CONT)

lemons, squeeze them dry, and fill everybody's cup to the
brim . . . with lemonade!

LAMB

Lemons?

DUCKLING

Cup?

CALF

Lemonade?

JODY

What are you talking about, Sam?

SAM

I told you, Jody, it's hard to explain. But look, everybody.
And listen. And learn.

> *(passes one chart each to JODY and, CASEY,*
> *who hold them up, and holds the third himself,*
> *all lemon side forward.)*

I have watched the Menagerie play long and hard. I have
watched the Menagerie play rain or shine. I have watched
the Menagerie play win or lose. And I've got the numbers to
prove it. I . . . have . . . *statistics.*

> *(signals JODY to turn first chart)*

Jody, if you would, please?

JODY

Sure, SAM.

SAM

> *(signals CASEY to turn second chart)*

Casey, if you could, please?

CASEY

You bet, Sam.

SAM
(to ALL)
And last but not least --
(turns third chart)
This is the full history of the Menagerie playing melonball
on Moore Farm. These are the team statistics, and I am your
team statistician.

CALF

Our statis-*what?*

SAM
Your statistician. Your keeper of the numbers.

FOAL
Numbers! Whoa . . . !

LAMB
Does this mean -- ?

DUCKLING
Could this mean -- ?

KITTEN
Do you mean -- ?

SAM
Yes! I have everything we need to fill out the application so
we can go to the Fruit Bowl!

> *(ALL except BOBBIE and FRANKIE go wild, an
> eruption of their creature SOUNDS, as they
> dance around SAM in joy and perhaps carry him
> on their shoulders. BOBBIE and FRANKIE*

back away, flummoxed. SAM leads his favorite
cheer --)

ALL except BOBBIE and FRANKIE
Horse! Goat! *BULL*, cow, cow!
EWE, nanny, *EWE*, chicken,
hog, hog, *SOWWWWWW."*
Moore Farm Menagerie –
Wow! Wow!
            (waving arms and jumping up and down --)
WOWWWWWW!

FOAL
If we're headed for the Fruit Bowl Tournament, we'd better
practice!

LAMB
Let's play melonball!

            (ALL except BOBBIE and FRANKIE
            enthusiastically agree. BOBBIE and FRANKIE
            look at one another in alarm.)

JODY
I nominate Sam for Scooper!

CASEY
Yes! All in favor?

ALL except SAM, BOBBIE, AND FRANKIE
Sam for Scooper! YES! YES! YES!

            (MUSIC, as ALL except BOBBIE and FRANKIE
            jump up and down and wave their hands to get
            SAM'S attention, with cries of "Oooh. Choose
            me!" and so on, while SAM is busy choosing
            and arranging PLAYERS, REFEREES, and

*MELON RUNNERS, and equipment is
distributed, FRANKIE and BOBBIE tip-toe
across downstage, trying to exit without drawing
notice. Just as they are about to escape offstage,
SAM sees them.)*

SAM

Bobbie! Frankie! Wait!
> *(MUSIC fades and ALL fall silent, watching in
> awe)*

Don't you want to play?

BOBBIE

Well . . .

FRANKIE

Yes!

BOBBIE

But you're not going to choose us . . .

FRANKIE

Are you?

SAM

Of course, I am.
> *(adding BOBBIE to one team and FRANKIE to
> the other.)*

I choose everybody!

FRANKIE

Really?

SAM

Sure!

                         BOBBIE
Why?

                          SAM
Why not? When I fill your cup to the brim, I fill mine, too.

                          JODY
I get it! Our cups are full! Of lemonade squeezed from
lemons! I get it!

                         CASEY
                    (to audience)
That's the kind of piglet Sam is!

              ALL except SAM and JODY
Yayyyyy!

                          JODY
Hold on there! These teams are not even!

              ALL except SAM and JODY
Uh-oh!
                    (Grinning, SAM adds himself to even up the
                    teams.)
Ah-HAH!

                    (MUSIC.   TEAMS embark on an energetic mime
                    of melonball maneuvers, as before, but including
                    SAM this time, while chanting, along with
                    REFEREES and MELON RUNNERS --)

                          ALL
Melonball . . . melonball . . .
Play it in spring . . .
summer . . . and fall . . .
Morning . . . evening . . .
noon . . . or night . . .

                    ALL (CONT)
we . . . love . . . to . . . play --

                 JODY AND CASEY
We love to play --

              SAM, BOBBIE, and FRANKIE
We love to play --

                       ALL
And we play it right!

                       SAM
All of us together --

           BOBBIE, FRANKIE, JODY, and CASEY
All of us together --

                       ALL
All of us together --
                *(a cheerful cacophony of animal SOUNDS and
                then --)*
YAYYYYYY!
                *(ALL freeze in a happy tableau. LIGHTS fade.
                MUSIC fades. End of play.)*

                    _____

www.ingramcontent.com/pod-product-compliance
Lightning Source LLC
Chambersburg PA
CBHW070937120626
46546CB00004B/1449